ESTABLISHING A FREELANCE INTERPRETATION BUSINESS

PROFESSIONAL GUIDANCE FOR
SIGN LANGUAGE INTERPRETERS

SECOND EDITION

BY

Tammera J. Fischer, CI & CT, NAD Level IV: Advanced

D1738877

Butte Publications, Inc.

ESTABLISHING A FREELANCE INTERPRETATION BUSINESS
Professional Guidance for Sign Language Interpreters
Second Edition

© 1998 Butte Publications, Inc.

Reviewer: Johann Paoletti-Schelp, CSC; SC:L; OIC:C; TCD V
Editor: Ellen Todras
Cover & Page Design: Anita Jones
Graphics: Patrick Fischer

This book is not intended to provide legal or tax advice. As conditions and regulations vary by location and change over time, the reader is advised to consult an attorney and accountant for appropriate and detailed advice regarding the specifics of the reader's own business. The publisher makes no warranties, express or implied, regarding the accuracy, currency or reliability of the contents of this book regarding legal or tax matters. The publisher assumes no liability for the consequences of actions based upon the contents of this book.

Butte Publications, Inc.
P.O. Box 1328
Hillsboro, OR 97123-1328
U.S.A.

ISBN 1-884362-34-6
Printed in U.S.A.

Dedication
To C.P.
Thank You!

Acknowledgements

The author would like to thank the following individuals for their contributions, support, expertise, and training, without which, this book would not have been possible.

W. Edward Ingham, Ph.D.
Ms. Cleo Arne, CSC
Ms. Judith M. Webb, IC/TC; CT
Ms. Liska Jewell, CI & CT; IC/TC
PS^2 Interpreting and Consulting Services
Columbia Bookkeeping
Mr. Patrick Q. Fischer
Mr. James C. McKnight, Jr., CSC
Ms. Sandra L. McKnight, CSC
Ms. Julie Gebron, CI; NAD Level IV
Ms. Debiah McKnight, CSC
Ms. Rebecca Robinson, CSC
Mr. Keith W. Schiewe
Ms. Darcie LeMieux
Mr. and Mrs. Owen and Leola Goans
Ms. Stephanie Stearns, NAD Level III
Mr. and Mrs. David & Judy Parmley

TABLE OF CONTENTS

Introduction...ix
Chapter 1: Certification...1
   Registry of Interpreters for the Deaf (RID).......................1
   National Association of the Deaf (NAD).........................4
   Texas Commission of the Deaf (TCD)..............................5
   State Quality Assurance Evaluations.................................6

Chapter 2: Legal Considerations...9
   Business Licensure...9
   Employee Status vs. Independent Contractor Status....12
   Tax Considerations..13
   Liability and Other Insurance Coverage.........................18
   Attorney/Client Privilege...19
   Interpreter Code of Ethics (RID).....................................21

Chapter 3: How to Set Up a Freelance System.................23
   Organizational Techniques for Interpreters..................23
   Marketing Interpretation Services..................................23
   Scheduling Systems..27
   Set-Up and Maintenance of a Billing System................28
   Information Required on Invoices...................................33

Chapter 4: Logistical Concerns for Interpreters..............37
   Team Interpretation...37
   Audio/Visual Presentations..40
   Cancellation/Billing Policies...41
   Confidential Case Notes...45

Chapter 5: Developing Yourself and Your Business.........49
   Characteristics of a Professional Freelance Interpreter....49
   Office Equipment Considerations...................................50
   Professionalism...50

Appendix A: Sample Forms...53
   Resume...54
   Bio Sketch..55
   Interpreter Request Form...56
   Facsimile Transmittal Cover Form..................................57
   Team Interpreting Sample Form......................................58
Appendix B: Language/Coded Communication
   System/Method Continuum Chart..................................59
Appendix C: Glossary of Terms...60
Appendix D: Index of Resources...61

INTRODUCTION

GETTING STARTED

The field of sign language interpretation is constantly growing and changing. There is a great demand for qualified sign language interpreters; skilled individuals are needed to maintain the profession's high standards.

A Guide to Establishing a Freelance Interpretation Business is designed to encourage all of you who wish to pursue freelance interpretation to set up a practical system that will facilitate provision of quality services, while allowing maximum growth of interpreting skills. The information in this book covers everything from types of interpreter certification, to self-employment taxes, to organizational concerns. This book will be helpful whether you want to work on a freelance basis occasionally or full-time.

If you are just beginning a career in the interpretation field, this book is an excellent resource that will allow you to become familiar with all aspects of the business of interpretation. Hopefully, you will find the excitement and motivation that will propel you to a professional level in a field that needs you!

One important aspect of self-employment in any field is the variation in self-employment licensure and/or regulations from state to state. For the purposes of this book, tax and self-employment information given will be confined to federal requirements mandated by the United States government, which apply to all states.

CAUTION: When setting up one's own business, it is advisable to have the professional guidance of either a tax consultant or a Certified Public Accountant (CPA), as well as that of a lawyer. The information contained in this volume is in no way a substitute for the services of professionals in the fields of tax law and/or accounting.

HISTORY OF SIGN LANGUAGE INTERPRETATION IN THE UNITED STATES

Sign language interpretation is defined as the process of receiving information in a spoken language (e.g., English), and interpreting that information into a signed language (also called a manual language) or signed system (e.g., American Sign Language [ASL] or transliteration).

In the early 1800s, American sign language interpreting originated in the educational system, at the American Asylum for the Deaf (later called the American School for the Deaf) in Hartford, Connecticut. Throughout the nineteenth century and well into the twentieth century, interpreters were not formally recognized as such, but were called "signers" or "helpers." They were usually members of the Deaf individual's family, teachers at the school for the Deaf, or church members who agreed to "help" in religious schools.

During the late 1950s and through the early 1970s, society's perception of Deaf people as those with a disability, began to change. Several new laws that facilitated this perception were enacted. The Civil Rights Act of 1964 prohibited discrimination on the basis of handicap. The Rehabilitation Act of 1973, Title V, Sections 503 and 504, required that various entities, from the federal government to employers of people who are Deaf, provide reasonable accommodation to people who are Deaf and/or disabled.

Also during this same period of time, individuals who had been providing interpreting services began to come together and seek out ways to standardize practices and legitimize the profession of interpreting for people who are Deaf. In 1963, interpreters convened for a conference in Indiana. This grass-roots group conceived what is now known as the Registry of Interpreters for the Deaf (RID), which now has national headquarters in Silver Spring, Maryland (see page 61). The original goals of RID were to: promote recruiting and training of more interpreters; maintain a list of qualified interpreters; develop a Code of Ethics for professional interpreters; and establish membership requirements and elect officers. Membership flourished, and in 1967 bylaws were adopted. By 1972, the RID had developed national certification for sign language interpreters. It also had adopted a Code of Ethics (see page 21) and had expanded to include state affiliate chapters across the United States.

In 1965, the first book on interpreting was published. Programs designed to train sign language interpreters began to develop in the early 1970s. Interpreter training programs (ITPs) give individuals the opportunity to gain basic interpreting skills. Currently, there are more than 75 accredited ITPs in the United States and Canada, of varying lengths and intensities.

In 1975, another law was passed that greatly impacted the need for qualified sign language interpreters: Public Law 94-142 (PL 94-142), also called the Education for All Handicapped Children Act. This law required that children who were Deaf and/or disabled have equal access to the mainstream educational system. Handicapped children needed to be educated with non-handicapped children, whenever possible, in the least restrictive environment. The mainstreaming of children who were Deaf increased by the thousands, as did the demand for interpreters.

Another type of certification began to be offered. This certification was developed by the California Association of the Deaf (CAD), and later was adopted by the National Association of the Deaf (NAD) for implementation. This certification system recognizes levels one (I) through five (V), one (I) being Novice, and five (V) being Master. This was a positive step forward, since the demand for qualified, certified interpreters far exceeded the supply (and still does).

The field of sign language interpreting continues to advance through the present day. RID, NAD, and local agencies and affiliates are making progress both in standardizing the quality of interpreting services and ensuring excellent communication facilitation.

By far, the most consequential legislation to affect the need for skilled interpreters is the Americans with Disabilities Act (ADA) of 1990. With the advent of this law, virtually every entity is required to provide accessibility to people who are Deaf and/or disabled. This law expressly includes the services of sign language interpreters as reasonable accommodations.

While many professionals in the field of interpreting work as permanent employees in educational settings, the majority of certified interpreters work independently as freelance vendors in settings as far-ranging as classrooms, theaters, delivery rooms, and courtrooms.

For more information about the history of sign language interpretation, please contact the Registry of Interpreters for the Deaf.

CERTIFICATION

PROFESSIONAL SIGN LANGUAGE INTERPRETER CERTIFICATION

Freelance interpreters work in a variety of settings: vocational rehabilitation, adult and family services, mental health, legal, medical, educational, and so forth. The skill and ability of an interpreter to effectively facilitate communication between individuals who do not share a common language, is essential. If an interpreter lacks proficiency, effective communication cannot take place.

In most settings, interpreters are required to hold either recognized national certification or a state quality assurance (QA) proficiency certificate, or both. While not all states use quality assurance exams to certify their interpreters, there are two national certifying bodies that are recognized in virtually every state—Registry of Interpreters for the Deaf (RID) and National Association of the Deaf (NAD).

RID Certification

The national Registry of Interpreters for the Deaf (RID) has been certifying interpreters since 1972. RID offers its test at numerous local testing sites around the United States and Canada to individuals **who are members of RID.** Local Testing Administrators (LTAs) are certified interpreters who have been instructed in how to administer both the written knowledge and ethics test, and the two performance evaluations. Not every state has a local testing site, or LTAs.

The RID evaluation consists of three parts: the written knowledge and ethics test, the Certificate of Transliteration (CT) performance evaluation, and the Certificate of Interpretation (CI) evaluation. As a candidate for certification, you must first take and pass the written exam. Then you have up to five years to pass the CT or CI performance evaluation before being required to retake the written exam. If you pass one or both of the performance evaluations within the five-year period, you are not required to re-take the written exam.

RID bases its exam on a continuum range. This means that the interpreter who wishes to pass the Certificate of Transliteration evaluation must transliterate in a signed-English fashion both receptively and expressively for the consumers on the testing videotape. Conversely, the interpreter who wishes to pass the Certificate of Interpretation evaluation must interpret into and from American Sign Language (ASL) both expressively and receptively for the consumers on the testing videotape. At the conclusion of the test, the tapes are collected, copies are made at the RID national office, and then they are sent out to raters, who assess the performance of each candidate. Finally, either a letter or certificate informs the candidate of his/her status. RID has granted a number of different types of certification over the past 26 years. These types are explained below.

<u>Standard and Specialty Certifications, Registry of Interpreters for the Deaf (RID):</u>

1. CSC—Comprehensive Skills Certificate. This certification was given under the old certification examination. Interpreter demonstrated ability to both interpret between spoken English and American Sign Language (ASL), and transliterate between spoken English and signed English or Pidgin Signed English (PSE).[1] *Certificate still valid, but no longer given.*

2. MCSC—Master: Comprehensive Skills Certificate. This certification was awarded to individuals who had passed their CSC. It was designed to screen out interpreters who had passed their CSC and had somehow received higher scores than their skill levels really merited. The MCSC is still recognized as a top certification level. This certification is much rarer than the CSC. A person possessing an MCSC has passed advanced written and performance testing at a master level. *Certificate still valid, but no longer given.*

3. SC:L—Specialist Certificate: Legal or Legal Skills Certificate (LSC). Interpreter must hold CSC or CI/CT certification and have taken advanced training for interpreting in legal/judicial settings. Has passed special testing in this field. *RID currently offers this certification.*

4. CI²—Certificate of Interpretation. Interpreter has demonstrated the ability to expressively and receptively interpret between American Sign Language (ASL) and spoken English. *RID currently offers this certification.*

5. CT—Certificate of Transliteration. Interpreter has demonstrated ability to expressively and receptively transliterate between spoken English and signed English or Pidgin Signed English (PSE) (Contact Language). *RID currently offers this certification.*

6. IC/TC³—Interpreting Certificate/Transliterating Certificate. Under the former RID testing structure, these partial certificates were given to indicate evidence of skill. These interpreters demonstrated sufficient skill to deserve certification, but did not score high enough to receive full CSC certification. *Certificate no longer given, but still valid.*

   a. IC—Interpreting Certificate. Partial certificate awarded when interpretation skills were worthy of certification, but transliteration skills were not. *Certificate no longer given, but still valid.*

   b. TC—Transliteration Certificate. Partial certificate awarded when transliteration skills were worthy of certification, but interpretation skills were not. *Certificate no longer given, but still valid.*

   c. RSC⁴—Reverse Skills Certificate. Partial certificate awarded to hearing interpreters when interpretation skills and transliteration skills were worthy of certification, but the interpreter did not pass the code of ethics portion of the test. Often this partial certificate was given in combination with the IC, the TC, or both.

7. OIC: C—Oral Interpreter Certificate: Comprehensive. This certificate was given to those demonstrating skill in oral interpretation, both expressively and receptively. This skill utilizes lipreading, speechreading, word substitution, and/or cued speech. *RID currently offers this certification.*

   a. OIC: S/V—Oral Interpreting Certificate: Spoken to Visible. Partial certificate awarded to interpreters who possessed skill in expressive interpretation between spoken to visible (orally visible) English. *Certificate no longer given, but still valid.*

b. OIC: V/S—Oral Interpreting Certificate: Visible to Spoken. Partial certificate awarded to interpreters who possessed skill in receptive interpretation between visible (orally visible) to spoken English. *Certificate no longer given, but still valid.*

8. SC: PA—Specialist Certificate: Performing Arts. This certificate was given to those interpreters with full CSC certification who also demonstrated advanced competency in performing arts settings. *Certificate no longer given, but still valid.*

9. RSC[5]— Reverse Skills Certificate. This full certificate has been given to Deaf people who have worked as relay interpreters. The process looks like this: hearing person speaks, hearing interpreter transliterates the message—Deaf relay interpreter receives the information and interprets it into ASL or the language system the Deaf consumer understands. This certificate has been especially useful when interpreting for a Deaf person with minimal language skills and/or multiple handicaps, as well as for foreign Deaf people. *Currently, this certification is being updated to become the Certified Deaf Interpreter (CDI) certification.*

NAD Certification

The second certifying body is the National Association of the Deaf (NAD). NAD offers its test for sale to any state that chooses to administer it, and that has a state chapter of the National Association of the Deaf. In many states, the NAD evaluation system is used as the state's quality assurance exam.

The interpreter is evaluated based on his/her proficiency in transliteration and interpretation, as well as situationally. The exam takes place before a panel of between six and ten individuals who are Deaf or hard-of-hearing, or hearing individuals who are interpreters. The candidate is asked a series of ethical questions involving common interpreting settings. Then he/she is asked to interpret for a series of six mini-assignments that are shown on a videotape. Between each segment, the panel rates the interpreter on all aspects of his/her performance. The situations require the interpreter to gauge the communication preference of the Deaf consumer (either interpretation or transliteration), and range in difficulty from everyday social-service appointments to legal assignments.

Once the candidate has completed his/her test, the evaluation score sheets are collected and sent to California to be tallied.

Shortly thereafter, the interpreter is sent either a letter and feedback sheet, or a certificate indicating his/her level of certification (I-V) and a feedback sheet. The five levels of certification are listed and defined below.

Level V: Master. Interpreters at this level have demonstrated ability to both interpret between spoken English and American Sign Language (ASL), and transliterate between spoken English and Signed English or Pidgin Signed English (PSE). The interpreter is qualified to interpret in all situations, including mental health, medical, or Felony A legal situations.

Level IV: Advanced. Interpreters at this level have demonstrated ability to both interpret between spoken English and American Sign Language (ASL), and transliterate between spoken English and Signed English or Pidgin Signed English (PSE). The interpreter is qualified to interpret in all situations, except Felony A legal situations.

Level III: Generalist. Interpreters demonstrated sufficient skill in interpreting or transliterating, but did not score high enough for Advanced or Master level. Interpreters in this category can interpret in general situations, including platform "auditorium"-type situations. This level of interpreter is not recommended for interpreting from ASL to spoken English.

Level II: Intermediate. A person at this level has received formal training or possesses equivalent experience in sign language interpretation. This person needs to build his/her skills and receive monitoring from more highly certified interpreters.

Level I: Novice. A person at this level is in the beginning stages of learning the role of the interpreter. More training is required for the person to upgrade his/her interpretation skills.

Texas Commission of the Deaf (TCD)

Individuals who are certified under the National Association of the Deaf hold certificates that are recognized by any state that has purchased and administers the NAD evaluation, **and** has a state chapter of the NAD. Texas is the only exception to this. The Texas Commission of the Deaf (TCD) has a five-level system much like NAD's. The primary difference is that the TCD test is more comprehensive and is administered on a level-by-level basis. In other words, an interpreter has to pass Level I before he/she can try to obtain Level II. This exam includes specific testing on a variety of different situations, and language systems and codes; it covers all points on the communication continuum. If an interpreter takes the Level III test and does not score high enough to be placed at Level III, he or she may still qualify for Level II.

The TCD testing system is recognized in other states, and like the NAD test, the TCD test is sold to other states. For more information, contact the Texas Commission of the Deaf.

Following are the levels of certification of the Texas Commission of the Deaf.

Level I Equal to RID Certifications: IC or TC or RSC (hearing)
Level II Equal to RID Certifications: IC/TC, IC/TC/RSC (Associates Level Equivalent)
Level III Equal to RID Certifications: CSC, CI/CT, RSC (Deaf) (Bachelors Level Equivalent)
Level IV Equal to RID Certifications: SC: L, MCSC (Masters Level Equivalent); Equal to NAD Level V
Level V Doctorate Level Equivalent

State Quality Assurance (QA) Exams

Finally, some states have their own state quality assurance (QA) exams. Sometimes QA certification is required in order to be a "professional sign language interpreter" in a given state. It is important to research which certifications are recognized in your state, and which certifications, if any, are **required** to practice interpretation.

Below are the levels of a typical state quality assurance evaluation.

Level V Equivalent to RID, CSC, CI/CT, RSC (Deaf); NAD Level IV; and TCD Level III
Level IV Equivalent to RID, IC/TC, IC/RSC, TC/RSC; NAD Level III; and TCD Level II
Level III Equivalent to RID, IC or TC or RSC (hearing); NAD Level II; and TCD Level I
Level II Equivalent to NAD Level I
Level I Equivalent to pre-certified interpreter still in training

On page 8 is a comparison chart of the types of certification, illustrating the equivalencies among the various systems.

[1] The current terminology used for this concept is "contact language." This is the communication that takes place between Deaf signers and hearing signers that are not native language users. The contact language is what evolves from their interactions and adaptations to each other's communication styles.

[2] CI/CT is the current testing system's equivalent to a CSC.

[3] IC/TC is not equivalent to CI/CT.

[4] This refers to the RSC given to hearing interpreters.

[5] This refers to the RSC given to Deaf relay interpreters.

CERTIFICATION EQUIVALENCY COMPARISON

TESTING ENTITY	RID SYSTEM	NAD SYSTEM	TEXAS SYSTEM	QUALITY ASSURANCE SYSTEM
WHERE TEST IS ADMINISTERED	USA Plus	USA	Texas & Arizona	Various Individual States
LEVEL/ CERTIFICATION	——	——	V	——
LEVEL/ CERTIFICATION	SC:L MCSC	V	IV	——
LEVEL/ CERTIFICATION	CSC SC:PA CI/CT OIC:C RSC (Deaf)	IV	III	V
LEVEL/ CERTIFICATION	CI CT IC/TC OIC:S/V OIC:V/S RSC (Hearing)	III	II	IV
LEVEL/ CERTIFICATION	IC TC Provisional Permit	II	I	III
LEVEL/ CERTIFICATION	——	I	——	II or I

* Please note, this is a subjective comparison chart that has not been developed based on a psychometric comparison.

LEGAL CONSIDERATIONS

BUSINESS LICENSURE

Business licensure varies for professional interpreters depending on the state in which the interpreter lives, as well as how the interpretation business is set up. It is recommended that any individual wishing to set up his/her own business contact the local chapter of the Small Business Administration (SBA) for its introductory packet of information.

For example, if you establish your own company with an assumed business name, a federal tax identification number, and/or articles of incorporation, you will be subject to laws differing from those pertaining to an interpreter who simply works under his/her own name while using his/her social security number for tax identification purposes.

Federal Documentation

Federal Tax Identification Number (TIN): For ease of business, or when contracting for protracted periods of time, federal tax i.d. numbers are often obtained. If an individual decides to incorporate, it is recommended that he/she obtain a federal tax i.d. number. There is no charge to obtain or maintain an assigned tax i.d. number. Federal tax identification numbers are not required of individuals working in a freelance capacity.

Tip: Federal tax i.d. numbers can be obtained via mail, phone, or fax machine. For more information, contact the Internal Revenue Service Center in Philadelphia, Pennsylvania, 19255, or call (215) 961-3980.

Required Form(s): Form SS-4—available at any Internal Revenue Service branch office, as well as many banking institutions.[1]

State Documentation

Assumed Business Name: Any individual wishing to establish a sole-proprietorship, partnership, or company, may wish to file an "assumed business name." This name must be an original name under which the business (in this case, sign language interpretation) will be run and identified. Business names **cannot** simply be the freelance interpreter's given name; however, the business name can **include** the interpreter's given name (e.g., Tammera J. Fischer, CI & CT; NAD Level IV, Ltd.). Upon deciding the business name, an assumed business name registration form should be obtained from your state's Secretary of State Corporation Division. On this form, registrants of the business are listed along with their signatures.

The business name submitted will be cross-referenced with all other registered names to avoid duplication within the state. Procedures included with the application will vary from state to state. Usually the state charges an application/registration fee; registration is renewable.

Tip: Request a copy of the completed registration certificate with your application. If you don't specifically request a copy, the Corporation Division will not notify you of final registration.

Required Form(s): An "Assumed Business Name Registration Form" is available from the Secretary of State Corporation Division in each state.

Women-Owned Business Enterprises or Disadvantaged Business Enterprises: When attempting to obtain contracts for long periods of interpretation work, or in trying to utilize tax advantages, individuals with female or minority status should consider application for classification as a women-owned or disadvantaged business enterprise. This classification can be especially advantageous when bidding on contract work, because requesting entities often look to fulfill Affirmative Action requirements. It is recommended that a lawyer be consulted if you are considering this status. To apply for this status, obtain an application from the State Office of Minority, Women, and Emerging Small Businesses. There is no cost to obtain this status.

Tip: The application is extensive and requires considerable documentation. The average waiting period for certification is eight months to one year. No rush requests are accepted.

Required Form(s): DBE/MBE/WBE Certification Application.

Articles of Incorporation: Articles of Incorporation can be obtained from the Secretary of State Corporation Division. The registration and renewal fees for incorporating vary from state to state. A number of differences exist between incorporating and registering under an assumed business name—including how your business is perceived from a liability viewpoint and from a tax perspective. For specific advice on these differences, contact a tax advisor and a lawyer.

Tip: DO NOT file both Articles of Incorporation and an Assumed Business Name Registration. If this is done, the Assumed Business Name will have to be canceled, and the registration fee is generally non-refundable. If the decision is made to incorporate later, obtain the necessary paperwork to cancel the assumed business name. If you want to request confirmation of the cancellation of an assumed business name, you may need to enclose an additional fee.

Required Form(s): Articles of Incorporation, Business Corporation Application form, and/or the Cancellation of Assumed Business Name form. This can generally be filed via fax with a credit card number on the application.

Local Documentation

Home Occupation Permits: If you wish to set up a business that is run from your home, it is imperative that you check with both the city and the county in which you live to find out whether specialized permits or licenses are required in order to conduct business. Home occupation permits are issued under two categories —Type A and Type B. Unless an individual has customers or clients coming into his/her home to conduct business, or unless the individual has employees, freelance sign language interpreters will fall under Type A permits. A Type A permit is defined as follows: "A home occupation is one where the residents use their home as a place of work; however, no employees or customers come to the home."[2] Once the application is completed and sent with the appropriate application/registration fee(s), registration will be good for a period of time, and is renewable.

Tip: After the application is sent in, the Bureau of Buildings will send an official permit to the business owner, which must be displayed in the place of business.

Required Form(s): Type A Home Occupation Permit Application.

EMPLOYEE STATUS VS. INDEPENDENT CONTRACTOR STATUS

It is not always easy to determine what constitutes employee or independent contractor status. Confusion may arise particularly when you are working for a significant period of time for one service requester. In general, the issue of control over the service provider, and how and when the services are performed determines whether or not a service provider is considered an employee or an independent contractor. For specific information with regard to state regulations, contact a qualified CPA, or a worker's compensation insurance company. The following is a general checklist of the components of employee and independent contractor's qualifications:

An individual is considered an *employee* if he/she:

- Is required to attend training sessions by the requesting entity (especially if the training sessions are given by the requesting entity).
- Coordinates his/her work schedule at the pace of the business, rather than at his/her own discretion.
- Has hiring/firing power, and/or supervisory duties at the direction of the requesting entity.
- Works within limited, set hours.
- Devotes all of his/her time to service provision to one entity.
- Performs all assignments at the employer's place of business using the employer's equipment (office equipment, desks, phones, etc.).
- Is required to submit regular oral or written reports to account for his/her actions at the direction of the requesting entity.
- Has travel or business expenses that are paid for by the company.
- Is able to be discharged by the company whether or not services have been rendered.
- Is able to terminate his/her employment at any time.

An individual is considered an *independent contractor* if he/she:

- Controls his/her own hours, and where and when he/she works.
- Is able to subcontract his/her work to others as long as the agreed upon result is achieved.
- Has the option to work for other entities (non-exclusivity to any one entity).
- Keeps his/her own office, phone, and business equipment.
- Schedules his/her own time to complete assignments.

- Receives compensation for travel and/or business expenses and declares them as taxable income.
- Provides his/her own tools to perform the assignment (For interpreters this would include certification, liability insurance, language assessment capability, transportation, etc.).
- Is able to realize a profit or loss as a result of his/her services.
- Makes his/her services available to the general public through advertisement (commercial business cards, separate telephone listing, etc.).
- Generally, is legally obligated (through contract or other means) to complete a given job assignment.

Again, these are very general guidelines, but may allow individuals to evaluate status when working with various service requesters.

TAX CONSIDERATIONS

For the most complete and thorough information about self-employed individuals' tax liabilities, please contact the Department of the Treasury's Internal Revenue Service and obtain a copy of the *Tax Guide for Small Businesses: Income, Excise, and Employment Taxes for Individuals, Partnerships, and Corporations; Publication 334, Cat. # 11063P.* This guide specifies all types of federal taxes that self-employed individuals must pay, as well as how often and at what percentage they must be paid. The following information is excerpted from this guide.

What Is Self-Employment Tax?

The self-employment tax is a Social Security and Medicare tax for individuals who work for themselves. It is similar to the Social Security and Medicare tax withheld from the pay of wage earners. You may be liable for self-employment tax even if you are now fully insured under Social Security and are now receiving benefits.

Social Security Benefits

Social Security benefits are available to self-employed persons just as they are to wage earners. Your payments of self-employment tax contribute to your coverage under the Social Security system. Social Security coverage provides you with retirement benefits and medical insurance (Medicare) benefits. For an explanation of the benefits available to you and your family under the Social Security program, consult your nearest Social Security Administration office.

Who Must Pay Self-Employment Tax?

If you carry on a trade or business, except as an employee, you probably have to pay self-employment tax on your self-employment income. A trade or business is generally an activity carried on for a livelihood, or in good faith to make a profit. You do not need to actually make a profit to be a in a trade or business as long as you have a profit motive. You do need, however, to make ongoing efforts to further the interests of your business. Regularity of activities and transactions and the production of income are important elements. The facts and circumstances of each case determine whether or not an activity is a trade or business.

Income Limits: You must pay self-employment tax if you have net earnings from self-employment of $433.13 or more in a given year. You must also pay self-employment tax if you are paid $108.28 or more in a year as an employee of a church or qualified church-controlled organization that elected exemption from Social Security taxes. However, see *Religious Exemptions in Publication 533.*

No self-employment tax is due on your self-employment income if the total wages and tips you received in the current tax year as an employee were $135,000.00 or more, and was subject to Social Security and Medicare tax (or railroad retirement tax).

Estimated Tax: You may be required to pay estimated tax. This depends on how much income you expect to earn for the year, and how much of your income will be subject to withholding tax. If you are also an employee, you may be able to cover your estimated self-employment tax payments by having your employer increase the amount of income tax withheld from your pay.

Self-Employment Income

You are probably self-employed if you are a sole proprietor, an independent contractor, a member of a partnership, or are otherwise in business for yourself.

You do not have to carry on regular full-time business activities to be self-employed. Part-time work, in addition to your regular job, may also be self-employment.

Some types of income, such as interest, may or may not be self-employment income. The source of your income and your involvement in the activity from which your income is received will determine whether it is self-employment income.

Independent Contractor: People such as lawyers, contractors, subcontractors, public stenographers, auctioneers, and interpreters [sic] who follow an independent trade, business, or profession in which they offer their services to the general public, are generally not employees. However, whether such people are employees or independent contractors depends on all the facts in each case. **The general rule is that an individual is an independent contractor if the payer has the right to control or direct only the result of the work and not the means and methods of accomplishing the result.** Income earned by an independent contractor is self-employment income.

Part-Time Business: Income from an activity you carry on part-time is self-employment income. For example, suppose that in your spare time you fix televisions and radios. You have your own shop, equipment, and tools. You get your customers from advertising and word-of-mouth. The income you earn from your repair shop is self-employment income.

Sole Proprietor: You own your own business and operate as a sole proprietor. Your income from your business is self-employment income.

Net Self-Employment Income

Net self-employment income usually includes all business income less all business deductions allowed for income tax purposes. You must determine your net self-employment income by using the same accounting method you would use for income tax purposes. You must claim all allowable deductions when figuring net self-employment income. Your net self-employment income is reduced by 7.65%, as explained later, to determine your net earnings from self-employment. Making false statements to get or to increase Social Security benefits may subject you to penalties.

If you have more than one trade or business, you must combine the net earnings from each business to determine your net self-employment income. A loss you incur in one business will reduce your gain in another business. You net these gains and losses only for purposes of the self-employment tax. Keep separate records for each business, and file the appropriate form or schedule for each separate business.

Deductions and exemptions: Your self-employment income should not be reduced by certain deductions used to figure your income tax. Specifically, do not use:

1. Deductions for personal exemptions for yourself, your spouse, or dependents.
2. The standard deduction or itemized deductions (from your income tax).
3. The net operating loss deduction.
4. Non-business deductions (including contributions to a retirement plan for yourself).
5. The self-employed health insurance deduction.

Figuring Self-Employment Tax

There are three steps to figure the amount of self-employment tax you owe.

1. Determine your net earnings from self-employment.
2. Determine the amount that is subject to the tax.
3. Multiply that amount by the tax rate.

The general rules for figuring self-employment tax are presented in the regular method discussed below. This method can be figured on either *Short Schedule SE* (Section A), or *Long Schedule SE* (Section B). However, there are restrictions as to who can use the short schedule.

Schedule SE: You must file Schedule SE if:

1. You were self-employed, and your net earnings from self-employment other than church employee income were $433.13 or more (or you had church employee income of $108.28 or more), **and**

2. You did not have wages (and tips) of $135,000.00 or more that were subject to Social Security and Medicare (or railroad retirement) tax.

Even if you are not required to file Schedule SE, it may be to your benefit to file it and use either "optional method" in Section B, Step 3.

Long Schedule SE (Section B): You must file Long Schedule SE (Section B) if you:

Have total wages and tips subject to Social Security (or railroad retirement) tax plus net earnings from self-employment income that are more than $57,600.00.

<u>Regular Method:</u>

Use the following steps to figure self-employment tax under the regular method.

Step 1. Figure your net self-employment income. The net profit from your business or profession is generally your net self-employment income. Net income is figured by subtracting all allowable business expenses and deductions from gross business income.

Step 2. After you figure your net self-employment income, determine how much is subject to self-employment tax. Your net income is reduced by the 7.65% deduction for figuring self-employment tax. Note that there is both a minimum and a maximum income limit.

7.65% deduction for figuring self-employment tax. Multiply your net income by 0.9235 to determine the 7.65% deduction (100%-7.65%=92.35% or 0.9235). This will yield your net earnings from self-employment.

Minimum Income. You must have earned $433.13 or more of net self-employment income before reduction by the 7.65% deduction to be subject to the tax (0.9234 x $433.13 = $400.00). If your net income is less than $433.13 before the 7.65% reduction, you do not have to file Schedule SE (Form 1040) or pay the tax.

Maximum Income. No more than $57,600.00 of your combined wages, tips, and net earnings is subject to any combination of the 12.4% Social Security part of self-employment tax, Social Security tax, or railroad retirement tax.

No more than $135,000.00 of your combined wages, tips, and net earnings is subject to any combination of the 2.9% Medicare part of the self-employment tax, until your combined wages, tips, and net earnings reach $135,000.00.

Step 3. Figure your self-employment tax as follows.

1. If your net earnings from self-employment plus any wages and tips are not more than $57,600.00, and you do not have to use *Long Schedule SE*, use *Short Schedule SE*. On **Line 5**, multiply your net earnings by the current tax year's tax rate. The result is the amount of your self-employment tax.

2.   If you had no wages, your net earnings from self-employment are more than $57,600.00, and you do not have to use *Long Schedule SE,* use *Short Schedule SE.* On **Line 5,** multiply the amount that is more than $57,600.00, but less than $135,000.00 by the 2.9% Medicare tax, and add the result to the amount of your self-employment tax (which is the current year's tax rate x $57,600.00). The result is the amount of your self-employment tax.

3.   If your net earnings from self-employment plus any wages and tips are more than $57,600.00, you must use *Long Schedule SE.* Subtract your total wages and tips from $57,600.00 to find the maximum amount of taxable income. If it is more than zero, multiply the amount by 12.4% (0.124). The result is the social security tax amount. Then subtract your wages from $135,000.00 to find the maximum amount of earnings subject to the 2.9% Medicare part of the tax. If more than zero, multiply the result by 2.9% (0.029). The result is the Medicare tax amount. The total of the social security tax amount and the Medicare tax amount is your self-employment tax.

Self-Employment Tax Deduction

You can deduct one-half of your self-employment tax as a business expense in figuring your adjusted gross income. This is an income tax adjustment only. It does not affect your net earnings from self-employment or your self-employment tax. You deduct it on **Line 25** of Form 1040.

For more in-depth discussions of "optional methods," refer to the *Tax Guide for Small Business: Income, Excise, and Employment Taxes for Individuals, Partnerships, and Corporations. Publication # 334, Cat. No. 11063P.* A current copy of this publication is available from the Internal Revenue Service, and contains the current tax rates for self-employed individuals.

LIABILITY AND OTHER INSURANCE COVERAGE

When working as a professional sign language interpreter, it is imperative to consider the impact one's interpretation can have on any given situation. This is of particular importance when interpreting in medical, mental health, and legal settings, although consideration should certainly not be limited only to those fields.

It is recommended that individuals working in these types of settings carry professional liability insurance for their own, as well as the consumer's, protection. In some states, or with specific referral entities, liability insurance is **required** in order to perform interpretation services in these settings. If you wish to perform these types of services, you should research the laws and/or policies of your state and referral agencies for accurate requirements.

There are a few liability insurance companies that have policies specifically designed for sign language interpreters. For information on these companies, contact the Registry of Interpreters for the Deaf. It is not required that the interpreter be certified in order to be insured.

There are alternate policies that agencies employing or contracting with interpreters may purchase, at a slightly higher annual premium, and with special fees for certifying "additional insureds" on policies.

ATTORNEY/CLIENT PRIVILEGE

Many articles have been written on the issue of sign language interpreters being forced to testify against or on behalf of Deaf clients for whom they have interpreted. The concept of testifying either for or against **any** party involved in an interpreting situation is in direct violation of the Registry of Interpreters for the Deaf (RID) Code of Ethics (see page 21).

In attempting to remedy this potentially discordant situation, several states with strong support from both the local Deaf communities and the interpreting communities have proposed legislation that mandates the extension of the attorney/client privilege to the sign language interpreter. It is advisable to check with each state commission for disabilities to find out whether or not this type of legislation has been passed in your state. NOTE: This type of legislation has not been passed in all states, nor has it even been proposed in all states.

If legislation is in place extending the attorney/client privilege to the interpreter, the general guidelines are as follows:
If an attorney and client are conferring, meeting, or otherwise consulting with one another, relying on the sign language interpreter for facilitation of the communication, the attorney/client privilege is extended to the interpreter; the interpreter **cannot** be called on to testify about any and all information and content conveyed during such an interaction.

However, if an interpreter and client are left alone, without the benefit of the attorney's presence, and thus without an individual possessing "privilege," the interpreter can be required to testified as to content conveyed during such an interaction (in which no individual carrying privilege was present).

Recommendation: Should an attorney or any other individual (e.g., spouse, member of the clergy) carrying privilege leave an interpreting setting, thereby leaving an interpreter alone without the extension of privilege, the interpreter should also leave the setting so as to avoid possession of content that could be subpoenaed and to avoid being required to testify.

Qualification of the Interpreter(s)

In legal settings, individuals present in various capacities during a legal proceeding can be required to qualify themselves on the witness stand before the court. Qualification is simply a means of establishing an individual's identity, professional background, training, and qualifications to perform his/her function during the course of the proceeding. It is in no way an attempt to extract testimony from an individual.

Qualification is often used when multiple interpreters are being used (e.g., a Deaf plaintiff is suing a Deaf defendant for rape, and the plaintiff has her interpreter, while the defendant has his). In addition to interpreters working as teams with the prosecution and defense attorneys, there could also be a third interpreter used to interpret for Deaf jurors.

Sometimes an independent interpreter will be called in by either or both sides in a legal case to assess the quality of interpretation provided by previous interpreters (which is frequently videotaped expressly for this purpose). This independent interpreter testifies as an expert witness. This testimony may seek to discount a previous interpreter's interpretation of past information. This may be a strategy on the part of a defense attorney used to gain leniency or release of a defendant based on the defendant's not understanding his/her rights or the charges brought against him/her, because an unqualified interpreter was facilitating the communication.

It is easy to see the need for skill and certification in legal interpretation, as well as the obvious need for professional liability insurance.

Generally speaking, RID's, TCD's, and NAD's Codes of Ethics (standards for ethical behavior) are courtesy codes (guidelines) and not usually enforceable in any state, except for specific situations. Do not fall prey to a false sense of security that the Code of Ethics will keep you out of trouble.

REGISTRY OF INTERPRETERS FOR THE DEAF INTERPRETER CODE OF ETHICS *

Regardless of whether an interpreter is a member of the Registry of Interpreters for the Deaf (RID), or if he/she is certified, the profession of sign language interpretation is set apart from spoken language interpretation because of its commitment to upholding and maintaining faithfulness to a professional Code of Ethics. Following is a condensed form of the RID Interpreter Code of Ethics. For a complete copy of the Code of Ethics, contact:

RID, Inc.
8630 Fenton Street, Suite 324
Silver Spring, MD 20910-3919
(301) 608-0050 V/TTY
(301) 608-0508 Fax
President: Daniel Burch

RID Interpreter Code of Ethics

1. Interpreters/transliterators shall keep all assignment-related information strictly confidential.

2. Interpreters/transliterators shall render the message faithfully, always conveying the content and spirit of the speaker using the language most readily understood by the person(s) whom they serve.

3. Interpreters/transliterators shall not counsel, advise, or interject personal opinions.

4. Interpreters/transliterators shall accept assignments using discretion with regard to skill, setting, and the consumers involved.

5. Interpreters/transliterators shall request compensation for services in a professional and judicious manner.

6. Interpreters/transliterators shall function in a manner appropriate to the situation.

7. Interpreters/transliterators shall strive to further knowledge and skills through participation in workshops, professional meetings, interaction with professional colleagues, and reading of current literature in the field.

8. Interpreters/transliterators, by virtue of membership in or certification by the RID, Inc., shall strive to maintain high professional standards in compliance with the Code of Ethics.

* Reprinted with the permission of the Registry of Interpreters for the Deaf.

[1] It is a good idea to make copies of all forms that are filled out and submitted. This practice will serve as a backup if something is lost or misplaced, as well as ensuring that a history of business actions is maintained.

[2] Taken from the City of Portland, Oregon, Bureau of Buildings Home Occupation Permit Notice form. Note: This type of permit varies widely from city to city and county to county. It is advisable to contact the local Bureau of Buildings, Code Compliance Department for state-specific information.

HOW TO SET UP
A FREELANCE SYSTEM

ORGANIZATIONAL TECHNIQUES FOR
INTERPRETERS

When setting up a freelance business of any kind, it is important to consider all aspects of the business, including: marketing
the service, advertising, bookkeeping, scheduling, situational
logistics, setting up terms of service provision, billing and collections,
and deductions of business expenses.

The way all of these factors are executed will have some bearing
on whether or not a business is successful. For example, although
you might be an incredibly skilled interpreter, if you were new to
an area and had no idea how to market your service, you probably
would be unable to sustain yourself. The remainder of this book
focuses on the actual setting up and maintaining of a freelance
interpretation practice. The following techniques and hints are useful to both certified and noncertified qualified interpreters who
freelance either full- or part-time.

MARKETING INTERPRETATION SERVICES

Before you can begin a successful interpreting business, you
must obtain the resources to market your skills. This can be done
in a number of ways, always remembering that the best advertisement of your skill is being referred by former consumers or other
interpreters.

When first getting involved with freelance interpretation, it is
advisable to meet and discuss with experienced freelance interpreters
what practices have been successful for them. Questions you

could ask include: Which referral agencies are reputable? What requirements do they have for interpreters interested in becoming independent contractors? This basic information will give a potential freelancer a general idea of standards that have been set within the professional community, so that the level of service can be maintained.

Interpreter Referral Agencies

Interpreter referral agencies exist all across the United States. In most states there are both state-run referral agencies as well as private for-profit and nonprofit agencies.

Some agencies cater specifically to those entities requiring sign language interpretation, and others include sign language interpretation in addition to foreign, spoken language interpretation. When deciding whether or not to contract with a given agency, make sure to research the agency practices, and to read and ask questions about contracts that might be required. Some agencies, while having good intentions, attempt to "add on" sign language interpretation without being qualified to offer such a service. Often, interpreters who are accepted as contractors are unqualified, and the interpreter coordinator is unable to match consumers to interpreters due to lack of experience in the field of sign language interpretation.

Be sure that the policies and pay rates defined in referral agency contracts are acceptable before signing on as a contractor. Some questions that should be asked before contracting through an agency include:

- What kind of certification is required?
- What is the pay scale for sign language interpreters, and does it vary depending on the nature of the assignment?
- What is the policy regarding team interpretation?
- Does the agency offer on-call services for medical or other emergencies, and if so, what are the requirements for interpreters who might perform such assignments?
- What is the cancellation policy for interpreting assignments?
- If I work for this agency, am I considered an independent contractor, or am I required to be an employee of the agency?
- If I contract with this agency, am I required to work exclusively for this agency, or can I work for other entities as well?
- How does billing work at this agency (for example, can I bill for travel time, mileage, portal-to-portal, parking expenses)?

- What is the net payment period for invoices, and do I bill the referral agency or the entity at which I performed the service?
- What is the background of the interpreter coordinator(s) and/or referral staff?
- What screening process is in place to ensure selection of qualified interpreters?

The responses to these questions should give a prospective interpreter the information needed to decide whether or not an agency is both a reputable and desirable place to work.

Introductory Packets

Another way to advertise interpreting services is to create introductory packets; these can be sent to a variety of prospective employers, including interpreter coordinators at referral agencies; entities that employ Deaf people; large corporations; state, local, and federal government agencies; public school systems; and colleges, universities, and so forth.

A strong introductory packet should include:

Cover Letter: This letter gives a general summary of who you are, what your general qualifications are, as well as what services you are specifically interested in providing.

Business Card: Attach at least two business cards to each introductory packet. When choosing a business card, make sure the card is unique and memorable. Having a logo that stands out often intrigues potential service requesters. Always list certification on the business card. Be sure to give a business card to both the hearing and Deaf consumers involved in situations.

Resume/Biography (Bio): Include a copy of your resume. A professional resume should be no longer than one page, and should include the most recent information available about your certification, education, experience, and any special skills you have to offer (e.g., tactile interpretation, cued speech abilities). A bio is optional, but can be helpful in highlighting special achievements, areas of expertise, and/or high profile interpreting accolades. (See sample resume and bio in Appendix A, "Sample Forms.")

Description of Services and Terms: It is helpful to include a brief outline of the services that are available, as well as your terms. Information that should be detailed includes: hourly rate (broken down by type of interpretation situation if an interpreter's charges vary), cancellation policy, billing policy, and travel time policy. Having this information laid out will alleviate potential miscommunication and misunderstanding. See the Summary of Terms agreement on page 40 for an example of such a description.

Who to Contact: Often, a specific contact person is unknown when sending out introductory packets to entities. However, brief research calls can result in a name; this will ensure that your packet is sent to the correct individual or department. Particularly with large entities, calls are commonly answered by a switchboard operator or secretary. Ask to be connected with the Human Resource Management (HRM) department. Quite often, the individual who is responsible for communication access is a member of this department within an entity. Potential titles to ask for are:

- Sign Language Interpreter Coordinator (unlikely, unless there is a **large** population of Deaf employees/consumers)
- Access Coordinator (ADA Coordinator)
- Disability Services Coordinator
- Risk Management
- Director of Human Resources
- Personal Services Contractor
- Director of Disability Accommodations
- Purchasing Department.

If there is no individual who is specifically responsible for procurement of interpreter services, it is appropriate to address a cover letter to: Director of Human Resources, and then To Whom It May Concern.

Business Phone Listings

If you have a separate business line, you are automatically entitled to a free listing in the Yellow Pages business directory under the heading "Interpreters/Translators" (or something near to that concept). This does not mean that an ad will appear in the Yellow Pages; it simply lists the name and telephone number. Advertising must be purchased through Yellow Page publishers, and varies in cost depending on the number of colors used and the size and shape of the ad.

TTY/Interpreter Directories

Contact your local chapters of RID and NAD. Often, state

chapters of these organizations either publish and distribute interpreter directories, or they can direct you to whomever does. Consider obtaining a listing in the Telecommunications for the Deaf, Inc. (TDI) national telephone directory.

Word-of-Mouth

The strongest advertisement is referral by Deaf individuals and other interpreters. Make an effort to team-interpret with as many different interpreters as possible. Be willing to be flexible and benefit from other interpreters' styles and feedback. Remember that interpreters are continually learning.

SCHEDULING SYSTEMS

Organization of interpreting appointments is a key component to being a successful freelance interpreter. In order to maintain accuracy, attention to detail is of paramount importance.

Scheduling Techniques

Appointment Books: It is absolutely imperative that an interpreter carry a record of appointments scheduled. Interpreters often call their appointment books their "Bibles." Appointment entries should include the following information[1]:

- Time and duration of the appointment
- Name of Deaf consumer(s)
- Name and phone number of the contact person
- Address/location of the appointment
- Job number or purchase order number (if required)
- Billing address.

Appointment books should be large enough to write a fair amount of information down, but compact enough to fit in a shoulder bag, purse, or briefcase. Keeping the book tidy is advisable; it is annoying to all situation participants, and embarrassing to the interpreter, if bits of paper and scraps are continuously falling out of the book.

Scheduling Services: Sometimes, especially when interpreters are referred to assignments by an agency, the interpreter must refer the entity back to the agency with which the assignment was coordinated, should further services be requested. Should the

Deaf consumer wish to have the same interpreter, he/she should contact the referring agency and request that interpreter.

Interpreter Request Forms: When taking down the information for an interpreting assignment, it is extremely helpful to utilize some type of request form. This form should list all the questions that an interpreter would normally ask in order to be prepared for a potential assignment. After filling out this form, in which all information is completely listed, there is little chance of forgetting to ask an important question.

These forms can be customized to match the needs of the individual interpreter. Included on the sample form in this book are the types of questions that should be asked. (See sample request form in Appendix A, "Sample Forms.") Specific logistics information will be covered later on in this chapter and in Chapter 4.

SET-UP AND MAINTENANCE OF A BILLING SYSTEM

Set-up and maintenance of a billing system is probably the most important aspect of running any kind of business. In order to keep track of monies paid to and expended by the company, there must be a system in place that is consistent and easy to follow.

Computer Programs[2]

A number of computer programs exist which specialize in accounts payable and receivable, as well as itemization of business expenses. When looking for a billing program, the following features should be included in order to meet an interpreter's needs:

- A chart of accounts for a service
- An invoicing feature
- A statement feature
- A customer entry feature
- The ability to print report summaries of various kinds
- Varying journal features.

Chart of Accounts: The chart of accounts allows the interpreter to enter business expenses of different types (e.g., gas expenses, parking, postage).

Invoicing Features: The invoicing feature posts the appropriate entries to the appropriate general ledger period; it is handy because it can be customized to each individual.

Statements: Statements are invaluable—especially if work is done in several different departments, although separate invoices must be submitted for each department. Statements are also helpful when collecting past due accounts.

Customer Records: Customer records allow an interpreter to gauge how much work he/she does for any given entity. This is very important when making decisions about how much work to take from any one company. Customer entries also allow invoices to be posted to each customer, and statements can be printed listing any accounts outstanding for any given customer. This is a great time-saver for interpreters needing summary information.

Report Summaries: Report summaries are excellent tools— especially when filing tax returns or paying quarterly taxes. Usually, accounting programs have various types of reports from which to choose. Another excellent feature of report summaries is that if there is more than one facet to an interpreter's freelance business (e.g., if there is an interpreting as well as a consulting facet to the business), then reports can delineate between types of income and types of work done.

Varying Journal Features: It is important to have different kinds of journals set up to track income. Journals are also the place where business expenses are documented. Because not all business expenses are paid for by check, it is imperative that an interpreter not rely solely on his/her business check register (or personal account if there is not a business account) to provide expense information. Journals allow descriptions of how things were purchased (by credit card, personal check, business check, etc.).

Handwritten Ledger Records

Depending upon whether or not freelance interpreting is one's primary source of income, an interpreter might decide to do all bookkeeping by hand. If this is the case, at least three ledgers or journals will be necessary.

General Journal: The purpose of the General Journal is to record business expenses that are incurred by the interpreter (or the interpreter's business). Allowable business expenses (tax deductions) are as follows:[3]

- Mileage traveled for business purposes
- Parking and gas expenses
  (gas expenses incurred during business-related travel)
- Professional dues and/or memberships
  (e.g., local RID chapter, national RID, NAD, local clubs)
- Professional subscriptions
  (*Silent News, Deaf Life, Community Ear*, the *NAD Broadcaster*, etc.)
- Licensure/testing fees
  (including certification and costs incurred for professional
  development/certification maintenance)
- Hotel/lodging expenses
  (including those incurred during convention attendance)
- Meals expenses
- Postage/mailing expenses
- Office supplies expenses
- Copying expenses
- Advertising/printing costs
  (e.g., invoices, business cards, letterhead)
- Capital outlay equipment
- Office rental
- Liability insurance fees
- Pager/cellular phone/long distance costs
- Business registration/permit fees.

It is advisable to divide the ledger into sections representing each of the above-mentioned categories, and enter expenses as they are incurred. Some receipts are not necessary to retain; you will need to check with the IRS as to which you must keep. Make sure that the general journal is kept up-to-date; it is easy to let receipts pile up, which is when confusion and error occur.

Invoice Journal: This journal lists all invoices sent during a given year. Invoices should be designed with all the information any entity could possibly need included. One of the stickiest parts of freelancing is collecting delinquent accounts, and it is even more difficult if an invoice is delayed due to information missing from it. For more information about how to set up an invoice, refer to "Information Required on Invoices" (page 33).

An invoice journal should have columns set up in the following manner:

Name of Customer/Date of Service Amount Due   Due By   Paid

Department of Voc. Rehab. 9/11/94 $40.00   10/11/94 10/3/94

This format includes all of the important information needed to track invoices that are outstanding or paid. Interpreters wishing to track amount of income earned at any given entity, should set up a journal for each entity. This is only practical if a great deal of diversity in interpreting service provision occurs, but frequently enough to warrant individual tracking.

Bills Journal: This journal is set up to record transactions that occur when paying bills with business checks. If an interpreter does not have a separate business checking account from which monthly bills (associated with freelance business operations) are paid, this journal would be unnecessary, and all bills would be recorded as expenses in the general journal. This journal should be set up in the following manner:

Type of Bill   Amount Due   Due By   Paid   Check No.

GTE Mobilnet Cell Phone $150.00   9/18/94   9/10/94   564

Bill journals can also be set up in a category-specific format as well. For example, all cellular phone bills would be recorded in one section, and all pager expenses would be recorded in another section.

Billing Addresses

It is helpful to maintain a file of billing addresses. If you are billing entities by computerized invoices, then you will already have entered all billing information into the computer, and thus you will have a "file" of all customers. If you are billing entities by hand, then it is easy to create a 3" x 5" card file of billing addresses. Dividers in this card file can be marked by headings denoting the type of business at which assignments were performed. For example:

Heading: Vocational Rehabilitation Division (VRD) Offices
Addresses: Salem Branch
                Hillsboro Branch

Central Portland Branch
East Portland Branch
Clackamas Branch

Individual index cards can be modeled on the following sample card:

```
Central VR Office
555 Anywhere Lane
Someplace, USA

Phone: (###) 555-3210
Contact Person: Ms. Jane Doe

Billing Inquiry Contact: Mr. John Doe
Billing Inquiry Phone: (###) 555-6238
Billing Requirements: AFP Number must be on the invoice.
Payment Terms: Should receive payment within four weeks
of receipt of invoice.
```

Having a system like this in place allows for smooth recording of payment and invoice receipts and submissions, as well as clear records for tax purposes.

Invoicing

All businesses must establish and maintain a billing cycle. This cycle is set at the discretion of the interpreter who, knowing when payment can be expected, is able to gauge at what pace and how much income will be remitted. If you rely on freelance interpretation for your primary source of income, setting up a schedule for billing is imperative in order to meet your obligations.

Invoices can be sent in a variety of ways: after each assignment; on the 1st, 15th, or 30th of the month; when pay periods are established by referral agencies; or in any combination of methods, as long as the method chosen is consistent and recorded in the invoice journal. See "Information Required on Invoices" (page 33) for specific information about the format of an invoice and information that should be included on an invoice.

Additional Forms

Many entities, especially those run by federal, state, or local governments, require additional forms in order to remit payment. These forms may be for the purpose of verification of the interpreter's presence, or just for the service requester's information. When performing any assignment, be sure to ask the requester whether any additional forms or documentation are required, and if so, how they might be obtained. Make sure that all required signatures from the service requester appear on the form(s) needing them.

NOTE: Any entity requiring additional forms should be willing to provide copies of necessary forms to the interpreter either by fax or by mail. If a master is provided for copying, the copying expenses are tax-deductible as business expenses.

INFORMATION REQUIRED ON INVOICES

The information that is contained in this section will help interpreters avoid one of the most frustrating drawbacks of working as an independent contractor: delay in receipt of payment.

Generally speaking, interpreters are classified by most service consumers (and payors), as "vendors." Often companies that receive other types of vended services such as purchase of stock and inventory, supplies, etc., have a set net term of 30 days. It is advisable to agree on the net terms of payment **before** provision of services occurs. This will allow the interpreter to have an idea of his/her upcoming budget. It is also a good practice to ask up front for any forms that will need to accompany invoices (sometimes forms consist of independent contractor certification, travel/mileage reimbursement, or verification of service forms). The following is a general list of possible forms or code numbers that could be required of interpreters at various different sites:

- *AFPs* - **A**uthorization **f**or **P**ayment vouchers. Often these are issued by state departments of Vocational Rehabilitation for individuals currently on VR caseloads. The required billing information that should be taken from the AFP and transferred to the interpreter's invoice is the **AFP Number**.

- *PCOs* - **P**urchase of **C**ontract **O**rder vouchers. Often these are issued by state departments of Vocational Rehabilitation for individuals seeking approval to be on VR caseloads. The required billing information that should be taken from the PCO and transferred to the interpreter's invoice is the **PCO Number**.

- *P.O. Number* - **P**urchase **O**rder number. Usually service requesters will either inform the interpreter of the purchase order number verbally or via fax prior to or just after the interpreting assignment.

- *Case Number* - Case numbers are often used for state case loads for Children's Services Division, or other advocacy type services. Sometimes caseworker signatures are also required in order for processing of payment.

- *Job Number* - Job numbers are often used by referral services that set up a job numbering system in order to track work per formed in a given time period. Numbering systems vary, and requirements related to inclusion of job numbers on invoices is also at the discretion of the interpreter coordinator.

- *Social Security Number* or *Federal Tax I.D. Number* - One of these numbers is virtually guaranteed to be required. It is, in fact, so much a part of billing in most accounts payable departments (especially those which issue 1099 summary income forms annually to its independent contractors), that often interpreters have their social security or tax identification numbers printed on their invoice forms or statements.

- *Independent Contractor's Signature* - Some agencies require that interpreters sign their invoices. This is especially recommended for those individuals who run their invoices off an automated billing system on a computer. Businesses match invoices to pre-filled out forms in order to prevent fraud, and also to verify the identity of the vendor.

[1] It is not advisable to write down confidential details of interpreting assignments in one's appointment book, since the information in an appointment book could be read by individuals other than the owner of the book.

[2] Computer program features will vary depending on the individual program and the type of computer being used. This book's recommendations for computer program features are based on the author utilizing PeachTree Accounting for the Mac for her business accounting. Other excellent programs exist for accounting, including QuickBooks and Quicken.

[3] Allowable business expenses vary from state to state. It is advisable to check with a CPA or Licensed Tax Preparer to find out what are considered allowable deductions. The list contained in this book is not meant to be comprehensive, but to act as a general guide of types of expenses.

Invoices can be distinct and creative. Individual logos are often marks of an interpreter's distinct personality and style (often the only one in a neutral profession!). Regardless of the style of invoice, information that should be recorded on the invoice must include:

SAMPLE INVOICE

Tammera J. Fischer, CI & CT, NAD IV
5555 Paradise Lane
Anywhere, USA

Phone #
Invoice Number   Social Security Number   Date_____

To:_____
_____

Date(s) of Assignment_____
_____

Time(s) of Assignment_____

Consumer(s) Name(s)_____

Location of Assignment_____
_____

Hourly Rate_____ Hours Billed_____

Travel Time_____ Mileage @ ? cents/mile_____

Payment Due Upon Receipt ▬ ▬ ▬

Amount Due - Thank you!

Signature_____
          Tammera J. Fischer, CI & CT, NAD IV

P.O. #_____

Job #_____

Other_____

This very basic sample can be modified to anything that conveys the same important message while remaing unique. Be creative!

CHAPTER FOUR

LOGISTICAL CONCERNS FOR INTERPRETERS

Due to the highly varied range of settings in which an interpreter might be required, it is nearly impossible to mention every situation that could pose logistical challenges. The primary purpose of the information in this chapter is to define and provide rationale for professional standards of conduct and technological needs that are often misunderstood by individuals not versed in the field of sign language interpretation. A second goal of the chapter is to provide models from which interpreters can learn to resolve potential pitfalls regarding compensation.

Please note that while these techniques have been successful, they are by no means the only ways in which to handle such situations.

TEAM INTERPRETATION

The concept of team interpretation is one of the most complex ideas for both service requesters and sign language interpreters to understand. Some notable quotes when asked, "What do you think the purpose of team sign language interpretation is?" have been:

- "To make sure that one interpreter doesn't get too tired."
- "To make sure the Deaf individual doesn't get tired of looking at the same interpreter all day."
- "To share the job."
- "To prevent repetitive motion injury."

It is fascinating to note how perspectives on team interpretation almost always seem to focus on making sure something **doesn't** happen!

Team interpretation is not simply defined as two interpreters sharing an assignment. Interpreters work in conjunction with one another as support or "backup" when providing services to a consumer. While some interpretation settings are less technical in nature than others, team interpreters rely on each other to provide missed information, technical vocabulary, assistance in voice interpretation, as well as physical relief. In a team situation, both interpreters are "on" at all times, not just the interpreter who is moving his/her hands.

The following information challenges traditional perspectives on team interpretation and gives some insight and rationale for why team interpretation **improves** and streamlines the interpretation process.[1]

When Is Team Interpretation Recommended?

It is recommended that a team of at least two interpreters be assigned to any assignment that is two hours (1.5 hours in some situations) or more in length. If the assignment is a recurring event or meeting, it will be **up to the interpreter** to decide whether the assignment will continue to require two or more interpreters.

There are several reasons to support team interpreting, rather than sending individual interpreters to work in two-hour increments and replace each other. Having several different interpreters over a period of time (for example, four interpreters working two hours each for an eight-hour day) is quite taxing for a person accessing information from a given source. Simply reading an interpreter for any length of time is tiring, but having a different interpreter every two hours compounds this fatigue, because the consumer has to adjust to interpreting style, interpreter familiarity with the content, and education of the interpreter as to specialized, negotiated vocabulary[2] which has previously been established.

In researching team interpretation with several freelance interpreters, it has been found that it is often difficult to gauge whether an assignment that is less than two hours (e.g., 1.5 hours) requires a team of interpreters. Several variables come into play and must be considered when trying to provide optimum services to consumers. Because of this "gray area," the author has developed a sample form that indicates whether or not team interpreters will be required; use this form when taking down information about interpreting requests. (See sample form in Appendix A, page 58.) Based on the information obtained from this form, the interpreter and the requester can determine how the assignment can be performed most effectively.

If, once one interpreter has been sent on an assignment, the assignment does not match the "sample form" information, it would then be determined that team interpreters would have been more appropriate. The interpreter should then consider the option of interpreting the full assignment for double the pay, or leaving the assignment after half the allotted time for regular pay.

It is very important that entities make sure they have considered all logistics when procuring interpreting services.

Team Interpretation Rationale

Some of the advantages of using team interpreters when the situation demands it include:

1. Consistency for the Deaf Consumer: As mentioned previously, Deaf consumers benefit through team interpretation, because they do not have to accommodate themselves to the variations generated by a string of interpreters.

2. Availability of Interpreters: If cost is an issue, service requesters sometimes suggest having interpreters work in two-hour increments rather than paying a team of interpreters for the total amount times two (i.e., for each interpreter's time). While this may save on interpreters' hourly fees, it decreases the likelihood of finding enough interpreters. For example, if an assignment is eight hours in length, rather than finding the optimum team of two interpreters to work the entire day (a total billing of 16 hours), some requesters suggest four interpreters working two hours apiece (a total billing of 8 hours). This requires twice the number of interpreters, and increases the difficulty of finding available interpreters.

3. Decrease in Incidence of Repetitive Motion Injury: The incidence of repetitive motion injury (RMI), carpal tunnel syndrome (CTS), and tendinitis is high among sign language interpreters. Because of the constant motion involved, working constantly without periodic, scheduled breaks can injure service providers. Repeated injury can result in inability to perform interpretation services, as well as other related physical problems in the neck, shoulders, and back.

Logistics of Team Interpretation

Working in shifts of 15 to 20 minutes gives interpreters a physical break, thus greatly improving the quality of the interpretation, while allowing the consumer to have the clearest communication access possible. **Break times should always be spelled out clearly and adhered to.**

NOTE: The quality of interpretation may begin to suffer after 45 minutes of constant interpretation. When working alone, substantial breaks (15 minutes or more) must be given to interpreters every 30-40 minutes in order to preserve the service level.

It is a reasonable expectation that, other than periodic breaks, interpreters should remain in the interpreting environment for the duration of a team interpreting assignment, regardless of which interpreter is working the last part of the job. Disruptions caused by interpreters leaving during the course of an assignment are unacceptable. If, however, an assignment is completed earlier than expected, interpreters should be free to leave the interpreting setting.

AUDIO/VISUAL PRESENTATIONS

"Oh no! It's a slide show!" Probably one of the most feared events for any interpreter is working in a situation which could potentially be set in total darkness. It is vital that information about such a presentation be given to the interpreter ahead of time. In the event that a slide show, video presentation, film, or overhead projector is going to be used, there are a number of ways to make the event accessible to all consumers in the situation.

Similarly, in performing art events or platform interpreting situations, there are ways for interpreters to have the best auditory access to information without causing any major upheavals.

Bank Lighting: If a presentation is taking place (especially a slide show, video, or overhead), lights can be shut off in various areas of the room in order to make the area near the interpreter visible.

Spotlighting or Specials: The size of an event and where it takes place will determine whether or not theatrical lighting can be used. Often a spotlight (with a gel over it to minimize glare) that is set large enough to frame the interpreter from the top of the head to mid-thigh, and at full arm-span, will allow enough light for interpretation to be seen. **This is not a suggested lighting technique for interpreters working in a theatrical performance.** Another possibility is to have a "special," or a light that is especially rigged for the interpreter in a specific area and is usually controlled separately from other lighting.

Video Presentations: If at all possible (for example, in a class-room setting or workshop setting), scan materials and syllabus schedules for indication of video presentations. If such videos were taped from public access or were recently produced by the Department of Education, there is a possibility that they have been closed captioned. **It is worth it to research this!** Make sure a caption decoder or captioned TV can be located, or find out if the videotape is offered in an open-captioned format.[3]

Auditory Access for the Interpreter: The echo and depth of a room will have a great effect on what kind of interpretation is possible. There is nothing worse than standing on stage or in a cavernous gym and having to sign, "I'm sorry, I can't hear/under-stand what they are saying." To offset this possibility, ask that a monitor be placed on the stage **facing the interpreter(s)** so that direct input can be accessed.

Make sure that there is no chance of feedback from other equipment. If the event is a large concert, wireless monitors are even better; they resemble headsets but are more compact. A clip-on receiver can be worn on the belt or put in a pocket. Technology is improving in this area all the time. Remember to speak with the sound designer or have your contact person do so to resolve your questions. Furthermore, **insist** on a test of the system.

CANCELLATION/BILLING POLICIES

Interpreters who freelance for their main source of income count on timely payments—even in the event of an unfortunate cancellation. Payment should be remitted in full unless a reason-able notice of cancellation has been given to the interpreter. It is extremely important that cancellation policies be laid out and explained in detail **before** commencement of the assignment. In order to enforce the policy, it would be prudent to fax a "Summary of Terms" form for a signature, or mail it if time allows. If neither option is workable, the policy should be read over the phone and the authorized requester asked for his/her agreement with the terms. Then document the date, time, and exactly what was said, as well as the name of the individual who agreed to the policy. It is unfortunate that this is necessary, but it is. On page 43 you will find a "Summary of Terms" form that could serve as a model for interpreters wishing to set up this type of verification system.

This document should also include the address, fax, and phone numbers of the interpreter. It is not necessary that this form be sent out every time one interprets. However, it is recommended that it be sent to any first-time client, and to any entity that is offering extensive hours of work.

Process for Collecting on Invoice

As regrettable as it is, it is all too common to find oneself having to chase down payments for services rendered. Sometimes invoices are put off for months. Professional interpreters can adopt the same protocol that other professional entities do when collecting money due them. The following is a guided tour explaining the proper process for collecting an invoice.

1. Once the agreed-upon net date for payment (e.g., 30 days) has passed, allow a five-day grace period to account for weekends or possible holidays.

2. If the check is still not received once the grace period has passed, call the entity and ask to speak with accounts payable. Inquire as to where the invoice is in the billing process: "Hi, my name is_____, and I am calling regarding an invoice for sign language interpreting services. The invoice number is _____, and the date of the invoice was_____. The amount was_____. I am aware that this payment is overdue, and I wondered when I might expect to receive it?"

NOTE: During any payment discussions/interactions, make sure to take down the name(s) of the individuals with whom you spoke, and the date, time, and content of the conversation, especially the date given as to when a check was promised.

3. If the check is not received either by the date expected, or 7-10 days after it was due (whichever comes first), send a second billing with an accruing late charge, and mark the bill **"Past Due."** Along with this billing, send a letter recapping the situation including the conversation with accounts payable, and the time

frame that was quoted for receipt of the check. Set a deadline for receipt of payment, and indicate that the next step will be collections. Following is a sample letter:

To Whom It May Concern:
I provided sign language interpreting services on (date). My invoice,
number _____, dated_____, in the amount of _____,
was due on_____. On_____, 199_, I contacted the
accounts payable department and spoke with_____ at
(time). He/She assured me that payment would be remitted by (date).
To date, I have not received payment for services rendered.

Enclosed please find a second invoice with an accruing late charge at
_____% APR. If I do not receive payment by (date), you will leave me
no choice but to pursue this matter to the fullest extent of the law.

Thank you for your time and prompt attention to this matter.

Sincerely,
(name)

4. If payment is **still** not remitted by the deadline, submit the bill to a collections agency, or consider taking the entity to small claims court. You can also choose to file with a credit bureau. For more information on options, contact a reputable attorney with experience in contract law and employment law.

Summary of Terms Agreement

To Whom It May Concern: The following billing and cancellation policies are my terms for provision of services. Please sign and fax/mail back to me as soon as possible. Thank you for your attention to this matter.
Name: Tammera J. Fischer, CI & CT, NAD Level IV: Advanced
Rate: 8 AM-8 PM M-F $_____/hour (non-emergency/on-call rate)
    After hours or S/S _____/hour (non-emergency/on-call rate)
    8 AM-8 PM M-F $_____/hour (emergency/on-call rate)

Explanation:
My hourly rates are stated above. I do not charge a two-hour minimum. I bill to the hour for any portion of time worked (e.g., if I work 1 hour and 15 minutes, I will bill for 2 hours). I charge $._____ cents/mile for travel over twenty miles. If I am required to drive one hour or more each way, travel is billed at 1/2 my

hourly rate per hour of travel time. Emergency assignments are billed portal-to-portal. If the consumer does not show up or the appointment is otherwise canceled, and I arrive for the assignment, a bill will be sent for the full appointment length. I bill for the entire time booked, regardless of if the assignment ends early; and will bill to the hour for any time the appointment runs over. Payment for services rendered is due **upon receipt.** If an invoice is out over 30 days from the date it was sent, a late charge will accrue at the maximum percentage allowable by_____ State Law.

Cancellation Policy:
- Whether or not I will bill for an assignment will vary depending upon the amount of notice I receive, and, consequently, the amount of time I have to find replacement work.
- I will bill the full amount for any appointment **1-4 hours** in length, unless **48 weekday hours** (2 days)[4] or more notice is received.
- I will bill the full amount for any appointment **5-8 hours** in length, unless **72 weekday hours** (3 days) or more notice is received.
- If a situation arises where I am booked for **one week** on a specific assignment, and the assignment is canceled midway through, I will bill the full amount for work performed, and the full amount for what would have been left that week. If the week-long assignment is canceled with **72-96** (3-4 days) **weekday hours** or more notice, I will bill in full for the first day, and half for the following days. If the week-long assignment is to begin on a Monday, and is canceled the previous Friday, I will bill in full for the assignment. If I receive **five weekdays** notice, the requester will not be billed for interpreter fees.
- If assignments are over one week long, the second (and following) weeks **are not billable** should a cancellation occur. Based on aforementioned formula.[5]

Example: I am booked for an assignment on Monday from 3-4 PM. I will need to be informed of the cancellation by the previous Thursday at 3:00 PM in order for the requester to incur no charge.

I understand and agree to the terms set forth in this document.

_____   _____
Service Requester   **Tammera J. Fischer, CI & CT;**
                                                                           NAD Level IV

CONFIDENTIAL CASE NOTES

There are several reasons for a professional interpreter to maintain confidential case notes. The main purpose is to use them as a tool that provides confidential documentation of events of note that occur during interpretation assignments.

Below is a possible format for case notes:

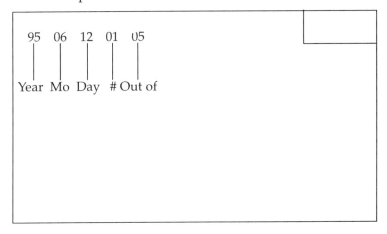

After each assignment, a 3" x 5" card is filled out using the above numbering system. The year is followed by the month and then day of the assignment, followed by the appointment number _____ out of _____ number of appointments performed on that date. The small square in the upper right-hand corner will be explained later.

One of the most pressing concerns when keeping case notes is confidentiality of all participants involved in a given situation. The point of these notes is not to record content of assignments, but to document any situational difficulties, unforeseen language or communication issues, billing problems, no-shows, self-analysis as to qualifications to perform future assignments in the same setting, altercations, etc. The case notes themselves contain no names, simply symbols to indicate: hearing consumer, Deaf consumer, team interpreter, and other language interpreter. Should names become relevant, the interpreter can refer to his/her calendar for specifics. The following page illustrates possible coding symbols:

Coding Symbol Examples

C = Hearing Consumer
¢ = Deaf Consumer
C̄ = Team Interpreter
C̲ = Other Interpreter

Symbols such as these ensure the confidentiality of the participants in the interpreting setting. In order to decode the case notes
and actually find out names of participants, one would need both
the interpreter's case notes and appointment calendar.

The upper right-hand corner acts as a quick reference point,
specifying which participant was the impetus for documenting
the events of the assignment. The following is an example of a
completed case note:

95 06 12 01 05	C

C was contacted regarding a past due invoice.
Second invoice was sent out after 30 days marked
"Past Due."C was contacted by phone after 45 days
regarding receipt of second invoice. C indicated that
original invoice had been mislaid, and requested a
fax of the original invoice as well as the second
invoice. Both were faxed today. Receipt was
acknowledged by C by phone. Payment is expected
within 15 days (6/30/95).

This tool can be very valuable, and is adaptable to individual's
personal record-keeping styles and/or needs. It is an excellent way
to maintain information for the purposes of self-evaluation, and/or
potential questions or problems that may arise.

---

[1] For more information about team interpretation by the author, see
"Team Interpreting: The Team Approach," *Journal of Interpretation*,
August, 1993.

2   Negotiated Vocabulary: There is not necessarily a sign for every spoken English wordor concept. Often a sign is invented or "negotiated" for use between the interpreter and Deaf consumer(s) during a given assignment. This is particularly common when interpreting in situations utilizing advanced computer or medical technology.

3   Any and all of these suggestions can be made to the service requester. It is not an expectation that the interpreter do all the legwork, but that he/she be perceptive enough to ask questions and incite the requester to action.

4   Weekday hours are defined as Mondays through Fridays, 24 hours per day, *not* business hours, which would be defined as 8:00 AM to 5:00 PM.

5   This policy has been developed as a compilation of policies in use in California, Oregon, Texas, Colorado, Alaska, and Illinois.

DEVELOPING YOURSELF AND YOUR BUSINESS

CHARACTERISTICS OF A PROFESSIONAL FREELANCE INTERPRETER

In addition to possessing interpreting skills, the successful freelance interpreter must have exceptional organizational skills and a high level of attention to detail. These two skills will allow a minimal margin of error when performing assignments for a large variety of entities in different geographical areas. The following is a list of qualities and characteristics that are common to proficient sign language interpreters; these are criteria to be considered when deciding whether freelance interpretation is really the right career for you.

- Strong interpersonal interaction skills on a professional level.
- Ability to maintain professional impartiality while remaining a compassionate facilitator.
- Ability to follow written and verbal instructions.
- General knowledge bank encompassing a large spectrum of information from which to draw while interpreting in various fields.
- Ability to team interpret effectively, and adapt to team interpreter's performance skills to facilitate as a team.
- Flexibility while maintaining a high standard of service and promoting progression of the field of sign language interpretation.
- Use of confidential case notes to document and maintain interactions and potential problems during interpreting situations.

- Ability to interpret/transliterate for consumers with greatly varied communication styles, languages, codes, and/or systems. (See Appendix B, "Continuum of Languages and Coded Systems Chart," page 59.)

OFFICE EQUIPMENT CONSIDERATIONS

Many technological advances have been advantageous for freelance interpreters. All of the suggested equipment listed below is clearly helpful in reducing time spent coordinating logistics, informing one of last-minute schedule changes, etc. For more in-depth information about any of the items listed below, contact your local office supply store or computer outlet.

- Fax machine and/or fax modem for computer (separate from home phone line)
- Access to computer e-mail (i.e., America On-Line, CompuServe, Internet)
- Computer system: either Macintosh or PC
- Cellular phone
- Alphanumeric pager
- Reliable filing system
- Personal/professional letterhead, business cards, and logo
- Voice messaging/call-forwarding services
- 800 phone number if serving a large geographical region
- Billing service
- Secretarial service or staff.

PROFESSIONALISM

The Registry of Interpreters for the Deaf attempts to set a standard for professional behavior of sign language interpreters. In RID's Code of Ethics, it is stated that "Interpreters/Transliterators shall function in a manner appropriate to the situation," and that, "Interpreters/Transliterators shall strive to further knowledge and skills through participation in workshops, professional meetings, interaction with professional colleagues, and reading of current literature in the field." While there are basic guidelines explaining these tenets, what does being "a professional" really entail?

Continuing Education/Professional Development:
Interpreters who strive to better themselves through educational opportunities and mentorship programs are enabling the field of

interpretation to truly enhance its definition as a profession. Certification is not the end to an interpreter's growth as a professional, but rather a base on which to build. With the advent of certificate maintenance programs, interpreters are being challenged to augment not only their interpreting skills, but their overall knowledge base, thus engendering versatility.

With the advent of CMPs (Certificate Maintenance Programs) for both NAD and RID evaluations, requirements are now being set on a national level for improvement and maintenance of excellent interpretation skills. Keep up with this and allow the progression of excellence to continue with passion.

Professional Demeanor: Professional interpreters arrive on time, are well prepared for the assignment, are attired appropriately, and have the skills to perform the task at hand. An interpreter's professional demeanor encompasses the general concepts of appropriate dress, personal hygiene, and polite attitude; in addition, an interpreter's professional demeanor, and ultimately, his/her facilitation skills set the stage for all interpreters who may interpret in a given situation thereafter. Interpreting service requesters will remember the one interpreter who appeared late for an assignment wearing a garishly colored shirt while chewing gum, much longer than they will remember the ten other assignments when things went off without a hitch.

Compensation: A separate ethical recommendation regarding compensation for interpreting services states: "Interpreters/Transliterators shall request compensation for services in a professional and judicious manner." This should include negotiation of fees and all associated costs prior to performance of an assignment; revision of contracts for services to be rendered (if any); special provisions for gratis services; as well as consideration of certification level, years of experience, and local-area hourly rates for interpreters.

Perception of the Field of Sign Language Interpretation: The individuals working in a given field make up the "profession."

If a general consensus about the professional role of an interpreter is lacking, the profession as a whole is degraded. If, as in the fields of education, medicine, and law, practicing individuals strive to enhance their realm of knowledge, embrace an ethical code of conduct, and provide excellent services as a result, what was once a mere field evolves into a profession.

Physical Maintenance: Physical maintenance of your most precious tools—your mind, your interpretive skills, and your body—will determine your longevity in this field. Regular visits to chiropractors and/or massage therapists will allow maintenance of body flexibility, range of motion, and correction of subluxations in the back and neck. This service is invaluable to interpreters who have limited choices of back and neck support, and are overly susceptible to Repetitive Motion Injuries (RMIs). Take care of yourself and prosper.

APPENDIX A: SAMPLE FORMS

- Sample Resume

- Sample Bio Sketch

- Sample Interpreter Request Form

- Sample Facsimile Transmittal Cover Form

- Team Interpreting Sample Form

SAMPLE RESUME

Tammera J. Fischer, CI & CT; NAD IV

555 Paradise Lane • Anywhere, USA
(503) 555-1274 (V/TTY)
Pager: (503) 555-4352 (V), (503) 555-7660 (TTY)

EDUCATION/CERTIFICATION

Portland Community College, Portland, Oregon
Interpreter Training Program - September, 1990 - June, 1992
Internship - April, 1992 - Closeup Foundation, Sign Language Associates, Inc.., Washington, D.C.
Associate of Applied Sciences Degree - Sign Language Interpretation, June, 1992

Hillsboro High School, Hillsboro, Oregon
High School Diploma, June, 1990.

National Registry of Interpreters for the Deaf Certification: CT (Certificate of Transliteration)
August, 1995
National Registry of Interpreters for the Deaf Certification: CI (Certificate of Interpretation)
August, 1994
National Association of the Deaf Certification: Level IV, Advanced
October, 1993

WORK EXPERIENCE

Staff/Contract Interpreter/Program Assistant, March, 1996 - Present
Columbia River Mental Health Services
Provided interpreting services, and coordinated interpreting services for a variety of mental health clients with diverse diagnoses including schizophrenia, ADHD, post-traumatic stress disorder, etc., as well as working with Deaf and hearing professional therapists. Services provided to a wide age range of clients, from young children to older adults.

Owner/Interpreting Services Coordinator, March, 1994 - Present
NorthWest American Sign Language Associates, Inc.
Own and manage a sign language interpreter referral service that provides sign language, oral, deaf-blind (tactile) interpreting services to individuals who are deaf or hard-of-hearing. Services provided range from communication facilitation on a day-to-day basis, as well as emergency, on-call services, and consultation for ADA compliance to interested entities.

Theatrical Interpreter, February, 1993 - Present
Tygre's Heart Shakespeare Co., Oregon Shakespeare Festival, Portland/Portland Center Stage, Tulane Summer Shakespeare Festival, Oregon Shakespeare Festival: Ashland
Provided translation and interpretation for productions of *King Henry IV, Part I and Part II, Henry V, Romeo and Juliet, Love's Labors Lost, Spunk, The Illusion, Jar the Floor, The Taming of the Shrew, Arms and the Man, The Tempest, Absurd Person Singular, Division Street, As You Like It, MacBeth, A Winter's Tale, From the Mississippi Delta, A Tuna Christmas, The Rivals, How to Succeed In Business Without Really Trying,* and *Masterclass (Portland Broadway Show Series).*

Interpreter II, October, 1989 - June, 1994
Portland Community College
Provided interpreting services at the college level when needed at varieties of levels and subject matters.

Freelance Sign Language Interpreter, June, 1990 - Present
Self-employed
Provided interpreting services at a variety of settings such as educational settings, interview situations, etcetera; including legal settings.

COMPETENCIES

Interpreting/transliterating/communication facilitation skills ranging from some forms of MCE to ASL; ability to work well with others; knowledge of Deaf culture including colloquial vocabulary; ability to benefit from criticism/evaluations; excellent organizational skills, professional knowledge; knowledge of effective methods of cross-cultural mediation/facilitation; Certified member and President of Oregon Registry of Interpreters for the Deaf, Certified member of RID.

SAMPLE BIO SKETCH

Tammera J. Fischer, CI & CT; NAD IV

Tammera is currently the Owner/Interpreter Coordinator for
NorthWest American Sign Language Associates, inc., a private, for-profit, interpreter referral agency.

CERTIFICATION
- National Registry of Interpreters for the Deaf, CT (Certificate of Transliteration), 1995
- National Registry of Interpreters for the Deaf, CI (Certificate of Interpretation), 1994
- National Association of the Deaf, Level IV, Advanced Certification, Washington State Association of the Deaf, 1993.
- Registry of Interpreters for the Deaf, Written Knowledge and Ethics Exam proficiency demonstrated, 1992.

EDUCATION
A.A.S. Portland Community College, Sign Language/English Interpretation
Certificate of Completion, Interpreter Training Program, Portland Community College
High School Diploma, Hillsboro High School

LANGUAGES
Spoken English, American Sign Language, Signed English

BOARDS AND COMMITTEES
- Local Testing Administrator (LTA) R.I.D. Certification Exams 1995-Present
- Chair, Certification Maintenance Program, Oregon RID, 1995-Present
- President, Oregon Registry of Interpreters for the Deaf , 1994-1995; 1995-1997
- Member at Large, Northwest Theatre of the Deaf, 1994-1996
- Planning Committee Member, Tygre's Heart Shakespeare Company Access Team, 1992-Present.
- Advisory Board Member, Portland Community College Sign Language Interpreter Program (SLIP) Program Review Board, 1991-Present.

HONORS: INDUSTRY RECOGNITION(S) & ACKNOWLEDGMENT(S)
- President's Committee On Employment of People with Disabilities Conference, NWASLA, Inc. won bid, and administered the interpretation services for this national conference (over 200 Deaf participants), May,1995.
- Closeup Foundation, Sign Language Associates, Selected as a staff interpreter, by video audition, for the Closeup Deaf Student Program, Washington, D.C.1992.
- Closeup Foundation, Senator Mark Hatfield, facilitated communication between Closeup Deaf students and Senator Hatfield, Washington, D.C. 1992.
- Governor Bill Clinton Presidential Campaign, Selected for television interpretation of campaign presentation, Portland Community College, Portland, Oregon, 1992.
- Erksin Bowles, Director: Small Business Administration, Portland Town Hall Meeting, 1993.

SPECIALIZED EXPERIENCE
- Theatrical Interpreter, Portland Broadway Show Series, 1996-97
- Theatrical Interpreter, Tulane Summer Shakespeare Festival, August, 1995
- Company Interpreter, Tygre's Heart Shakespeare Company, Portland, Oregon, 1993-1995.
- Interpreter, Oregon Shakespeare Festival: Portland,/Portland Center Stage, Portland, Oregon, and Oregon Shakespeare Festival Ashland, 1993-Present.
- Interpreter, Portland Community College Telecourses, Portland, Oregon, 1993.
- Interpreter, Portland Community College, Portland, Oregon, 1989-1994.
- Interpreter, Portland State University, Portland, Oregon, 1992-1993.
- Interpreter, Clackamas Community College, Oregon City, Oregon,1992.
- Senior ASL Relay Operator, Oregon Relay Service, Portland, Oregon, 1990-1992.

INTERPRETER EDUCATION
- Instructor: Portland Community College Sign Language Interpretation Program (SLIP) Community Interpreting Internship, Spring Term, 1996.

PROFESSIONAL MEMBERSHIPS
- Registry of Interpreters for the Deaf, Certified Member, 1991-Present
- Oregon Registry of Interpreters for the Deaf, Certified Member, 1990- Present.
- Washington State Association of the Deaf, Certified Member, 1994-Present

PUBLICATIONS
- Team Interpreting: the Team Approach, *Journal of Interpretation*, August, 1993.
- Team Interpreting: the Team Approach, *RID Views*, April 1994.
- "Establishing A Freelance Interpretation Business: Professional Guidance for Sign Language Interpreters" May, 1995.

SAMPLE INTERPRETER REQUEST FORM

INTERPRETER REQUEST FORM

Form Filled Out By:_____

Date:_____ Time:_____

Requester Name:_____ Phone Number:_____

Company Name:_____ FAX Number:_____

Contact Person:_____ Phone Number:_____

Billing Address:_____

_____

Deaf Consumer(s):_____

_____

Date(s) of Appointment(s):_____

_____

Time(s) of Appointment(s): From:_____ To:_____

Location of Assignment:_____

_____

Purchase Order Number:_____

Assignment Type:_____

_____

Type of Interpreting Requested: ASL ❑   Transliteration ❑   MLS ❑   Oral ❑   Deaf Blind ❑

Special Requests:_____

_____

Fee:_____

_____

Cancellation Policy Sent/Faxed ❑ Date:_____ Time:_____

Confirmations Sent   ❑ Date:_____ Time:_____

SAMPLE FACSIMILE TRANSMITTAL COVER FORM

FACSIMILE TRANSMITTAL COVER

From:_____   Date:_____

_____   Voice Telephone: _____

_____   TTY: _____

_____   FAX: _____

Please deliver this FAX to:

    Attention:_____   FAX Number:_____

    Company:_____   Telephone:_____

Subject:_____

Pages:_____Including this cover page.

Message

ADDRESS: _____

PHONE: _____   TTY: _____   FAX: _____

TEAM INTERPRETING SAMPLE FORM

1. How long is the total interpreting assignment, from start to finish?

2. What kind of interpretation is required (e.g., ASL, Oral, PSE, SEE, Tactile)?

3. Does the content of the assignment contain a great deal of technical vocabulary, acronyms, and/or specific field-related references?

4. Will technical information, outlines, curriculum, and/or presentations be available for review prior to the interpreting assignment? (Preparation is billed at half the interpreter's hourly rate, per hour.)

5. Will there be any reading from text during the assignment?

6. Are any breaks scheduled during the course of the assignment, or is it constant/nonstop? Define the amount of break time the interpreter requires.

7. Will there be any media presentations during the assignment (i.e., slides, videotapes that are not captioned, films, or audio media)?

8. Is a Deaf individual or individuals presenting during the assignment?

9. Will the assignment be videotaped?

10. Does/do the client(s) have any special needs or requirements (for example, color of clothing, male/female interpreter preference, tunnel vision)?

11. Is the interpreting assignment of a sensitive nature, or potentially volatile (e.g. counseling)?

APPENDIX B: LANGUAGE/CODED COMMUNICATION SYSTEM/METHOD CONTINUUM CHART

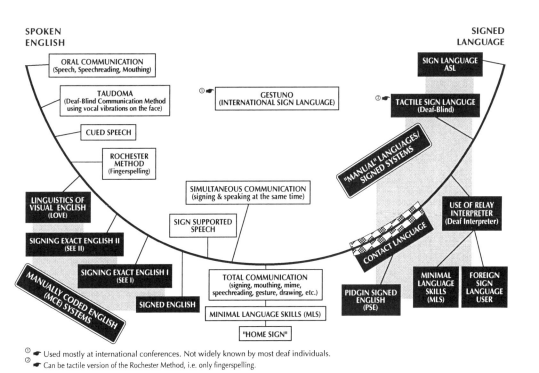

SPOKEN ENGLISH

SIGNED LANGUAGE

ORAL COMMUNICATION
(Speech, Speechreading, Mouthing)

SIGN LANGUAGE ASL

TAUDOMA
(Deaf-Blind Communication Method using vocal vibrations on the face)

① ☞ GESTUNO
(INTERNATIONAL SIGN LANGUAGE)

② ☞ TACTILE SIGN LANGUGE
(Deaf-Blind)

CUED SPEECH

ROCHESTER METHOD
(Fingerspelling)

"MANUAL" LANGUAGES/ SIGNED SYSTEMS

LINGUISTICS OF VISUAL ENGLISH
(LOVE)

SIMULTANEOUS COMMUNICATION
(signing & speaking at the same time)

USE OF RELAY INTERPRETER
(Deaf Interpreter)

SIGNING EXACT ENGLISH II
(SEE II)

SIGN SUPPORTED SPEECH

CONTACT LANGUAGE

SIGNING EXACT ENGLISH I
(SEE I)

TOTAL COMMUNICATION
(signing, mouthing, mime, speechreading, gesture, drawing, etc.)

MINIMAL LANGUAGE SKILLS
(MLS)

FOREIGN SIGN LANGUAGE USER

MANUALLY CODED ENGLISH (MCE) SYSTEMS

SIGNED ENGLISH

PIDGIN SIGNED ENGLISH
(PSE)

MINIMAL LANGUAGE SKILLS (MLS)

"HOME SIGN"

① ☞ Used mostly at international conferences. Not widely known by most deaf individuals.
② ☞ Can be tactile version of the Rochester Method, i.e. only fingerspelling.

APPENDIX C: GLOSSARY OF TERMS

Interpretation: The process of interpreting from signed or spoken English to American Sign Language (ASL), both expressively and receptively.

Transliteration: The process of transliterating from spoken English to signed, manually coded, or visual English or contact language.

Continuum Range: A scale used to determine proficiency in types of interpretation/transliteration skills. A strong transliterator would possess skills in facilitating communication taking place at the signed/spoken English end of the continuum, while a strong interpreter would possess skills in facilitating communication taking place at the ASL end of the continuum.

ASL: American Sign Language

TCD: Texas Commission of the Deaf

MBE: Minority Business Enterprise

WBE: Women-Owned Business Enterprise

DBE: Disadvantaged Business Enterprise

APPENDIX D: INDEX OF RESOURCES

Registry of Interpreters for the Deaf (RID)
8630 Fenton Street, Suite 324
Silver Spring, Maryland 20910-3919
(301) 608-0050 V/TTY
(301) 608-0508 Fax
President: Daniel Burch

National Association of the Deaf (NAD)
814 Thayer Avenue
Silver Spring, Maryland 20910
(301) 587-1789 TTY
(301) 587-1788 V
(301) 587-1791 Fax
Executive Director: Nancy J. Bloch
Bookstore: (301) 587-5262 V
          (301) 587-5263 TTY
          (301) 587-4873 Fax

California Center for Law & the Deaf (CALCLAD)
14895 E. 14th Street, Suite 220
San Leandro, CA 94578
(510) 483-0922 V/TTY
(510) 483-0967 Fax
Legal Director: Ken Kresse

National Center for Law & the Deaf (NCLD)
Gallaudet University
800 Florida Avenue NE
Washington, D.C. 20002
(202) 651-5373 V/TTY
(202) 651-5381 Fax
Legal Director: Sy Dubow

Texas Commission of the Deaf (TCD)
4800 North Lamar, Suite 310
P.O. Box 12904
Austin, Texas 78756
(512) 451-8494 TTY/V
(512) 451-9316 Fax

The National Theatre of the Deaf (NTD)
P. O. Box 659
Chester, Connecticut 06412
(203) 526-4974 TTY
(203) 526-4971 V
(203) 526-0066 Fax
Artistic Directors: Camille L. Jeter, Will Rhys

Greater Los Angeles Council on Deafness (GLAD)
2222 Laverna Avenue
Los Angeles, California 90041
(213) 478-8000 TTY/V
(213) 478-8016 Fax
Executive Director: Marcella Meyer

Deaf Counseling, Advocacy, and Referral Agency (DCARA)
14895 E. 14th Strret, Suite 200
San Leandro, CA 94578
(510) 483-0753 V / TTY
(510) 483-0778 Fax

NorthWest American Sign Language Associates, Inc.
16141 NW Energia Street
Portland, Oregon 97229
(503) 629-5788 V
(800) 275-1541 V
(503) 629-8800 TTY
(503) 690-0941 Fax
President: Tammera Fischer

P-S Squared Interpreting and Consultation Services
2625 SE Hawthorne Blvd.
Portland, Oregon 97214
(503) 236-3656 V
(503) 236-2826 TTY
(503) 236-3262
President: Johann Paoletti-Schelp

For In-Depth Information about Visual Telecommunications, please contact:

Telecommunications for the Deaf, Inc. (TDI)
8719 Colesville Road, Suite 300
Silver Spring, Maryland 20910
(301) 589-3006 TTY
(301) 589-3786 V
(301) 589-3797 Fax

NOTES:

NOTES:

NOTES:

NOTES:

NOTES: